D1141230

Ocean Explorer!

Angela Royston

Published 2011 by
A&C Black Publishers Ltd.
36 Soho Square, London, W1D 3QY

www.acblack.com

ISBN   HB 978-1-4081-3375-0
       PB 978-1-4081-3374-3

Text copyright © 2010 Angela Royston

This book is produced using paper that is made from wood grown in managed, sustainable forests. It is natural, renewable and recyclable. The logging and manufacturing processes conform to the environmental regulations of the country of origin.

Produced for A&C Black by Calcium. www.calciumcreative.co.uk

Printed and bound in China by C&C Offset Printing Co.

All the internet addresses given in this book were correct at the time of going to press. The author and publishers regret any inconvenience caused if addresses have changed or sites have ceased to exist, but can accept no responsibility for any such changes.

Acknowledgements

The publishers would like to thank the following for their kind permission to reproduce their photographs:

Cover: Shutterstock
Pages: Dreamstime: Amandamhanna 20, Michael Ansell 10, Alain Lacroix 21, Ne_fall_foliage 11; Photolibrary: Splashdown Direct 18, Volvox volvox 15; Shutterstock: Subbotina Anna 4, Rich Carey 5, Steven Gibson 7, Idreamphoto 6, Knumina 8, Levent Konuk 12, Joze Maucec 16, NatalieJean 17, Nautilus Media 19, Nataliya Taratunina 9, Tonobalaguerf 13, Joanna Zopoth-Lipiejko 14.

Contents

Dive In

The ocean is full of amazing creatures. I saw lots on my **dive**.

Undersea horse

First I saw a sea horse. Its head looks a bit like a horse's head!

Sea horses have long, curly tails.

4

My dive photos

I used a special camera to take photos. It works underwater.

Giddy up!

Seabed Swimmer

Next I saw a turtle swimming across the **seabed**. It was looking for **shellfish** to eat.

Tough stuff
A turtle has a tough **shell** around its body.

A turtle uses its **flippers** to swim.

Flipper ———○

Shell

In hiding

A turtle lays her eggs on the beach. They **hatch** into baby turtles.

I'm hungry!

Sandy Star

Then I saw a starfish on the seabed. It had five arms and looked like a star.

Ooops!
One of its arms fell off when I picked the starfish up! Luckily, another arm will soon grow.

I'm hiding

No head

A starfish has no head. Its eyes are at the end of its arms.

Starfish try to hide under the sand.

9

Ink Bomb!

Then I saw a long, wavy **tentacle**. It belonged to an octopus.

Ink attack

When I tried to touch the octopus, it squirted me with black **ink**. Then it zoomed away.

Tentacle ———

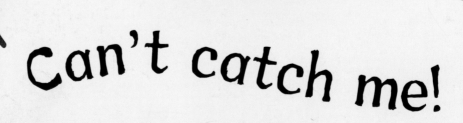

Can't catch me!

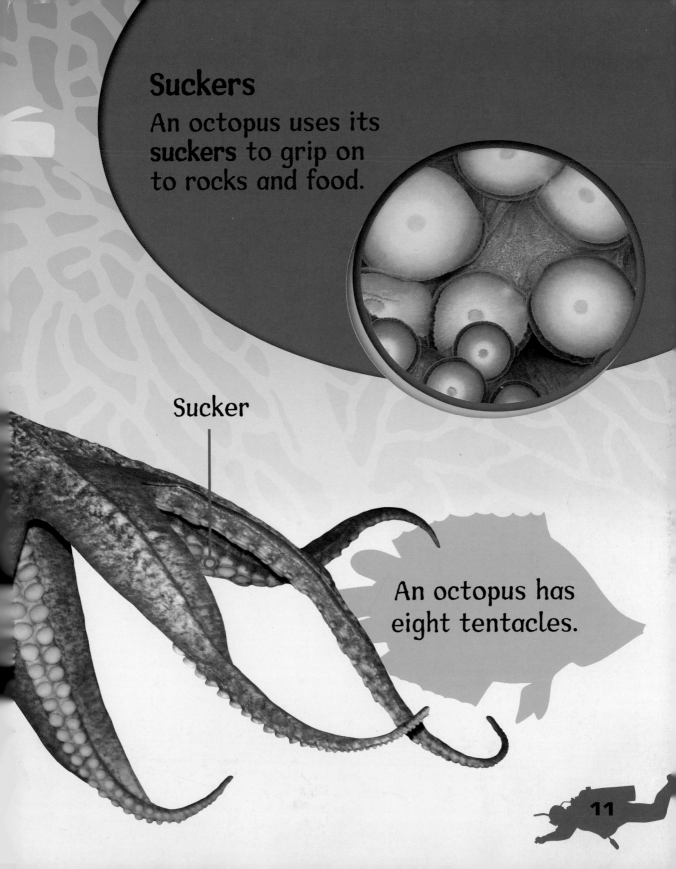

Suckers

An octopus uses its **suckers** to grip on to rocks and food.

Sucker

An octopus has eight tentacles.

Fantastic Fish

I saw lots of fish swimming below me. They were many different shapes and colours.

Stripey swimmers

Many kinds of colourful fish swim around **coral reefs**. I liked the stripey ones best.

Some fish are super-stripey.

Long sword

A swordfish uses its 'sword' to kill fish to eat.

Look at me!

Crab Attack

Next I spotted a crab. It crept out from under a stone. I dived down to get a closer look.

Crab grab

The crab had eight legs and two big claws. It grabbed me with one of its claws!

Eye

Claw

Watch out

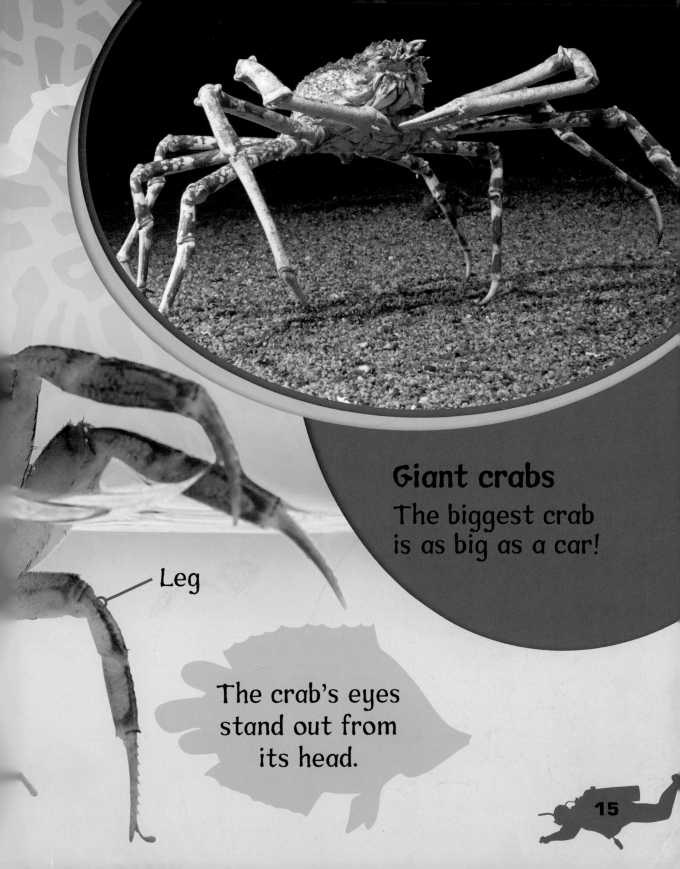

Giant crabs

The biggest crab
is as big as a car!

Leg

The crab's eyes
stand out from
its head.

Super Spikey

Some sea urchins were clinging to the rocks. Sea urchins look like plants, but they are animals.

Ouch!

Sea urchins are covered with sharp spikes. I was careful not to step on one!

Some sea urchins have **poison** in their spikes.

Shells and spikes

A sea urchin's shell is covered in spikes.

Don't step on me!

Giant Shark!

As I swam back to the surface, a basking shark swam by. It is the second biggest shark in the world.

Big mouth

A basking shark has a huge mouth, but I wasn't afraid. It doesn't attack people.

Open wide

Basking sharks eat tiny animals.

Spotty shark

This spotted fish is a small shark. It is called a dogfish.

Stinging Jellyfish

As I swam to the beach, I saw a stinging jellyfish. Its body was made of jelly and it had long tentacles.

Deadly sting

The tentacles have **poisonous** stings. The stings of some jellyfish can kill you!

Wibble wobble

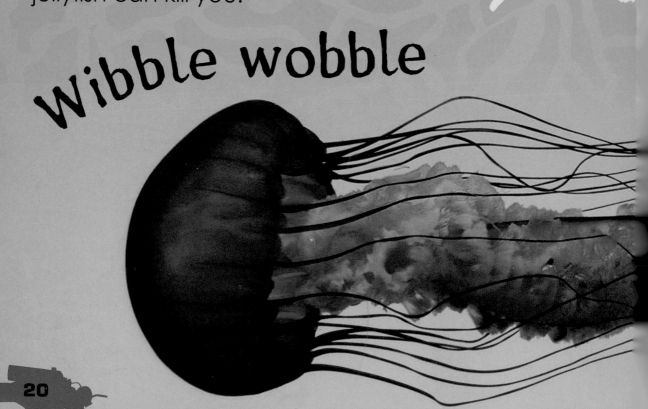

Baby jellyfish

Jellyfish are tiny at first. They float and feed in the sea.

Tentacle

This jellyfish is shaped like an umbrella.

Glossary

coral reefs structures that feel like rock but are made of millions of tiny sea animals

dive going down beneath the surface of the water

flippers wide, flat body parts used for swimming. Some sea animals have flippers.

hatch to break out of an egg

ink liquid that an octopus squirts to protect itself

poison something that is harmful if eaten or if it enters your blood

seabed ground at the bottom of the sea

shell hard cover that protects an animal's body

shellfish sea creatures that have a shell

suckers parts that grip on to rocks or other surfaces

tentacle long feeler that a sea animal uses to move and feel. Some tentacles contain stings.

Further Reading

Websites

This website tells you about several of the sea animals in this book. Go down to 'Invertebrates' and click on the animals in the list. You can find them at:
http://animals.nationalgeographic.com/animals/facts

Play games and find out more about sea creatures at:
http://learnenglishkids.britishcouncil.org/category/ general-themes/sea-animals

Books

Planet Animal: Under the Sea by Anita Ganeri, Carlton Books (2009).

See Under the Sea by Kate Daynes, Usborne (2008).

Under the Sea by Fiona Patchett, Usborne (2002).

Index